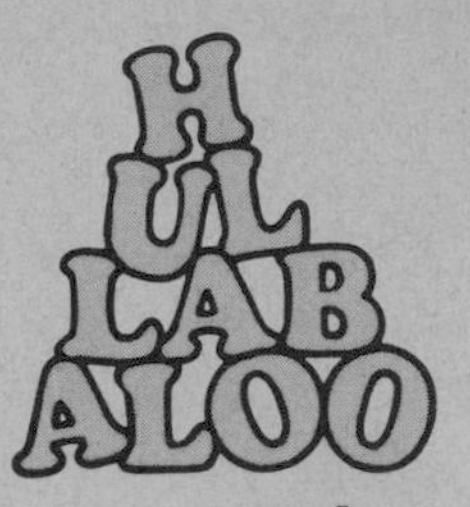

The Hullabaloo Discothèque Dance Book

The Hullabaloo Discothèque Dance Book

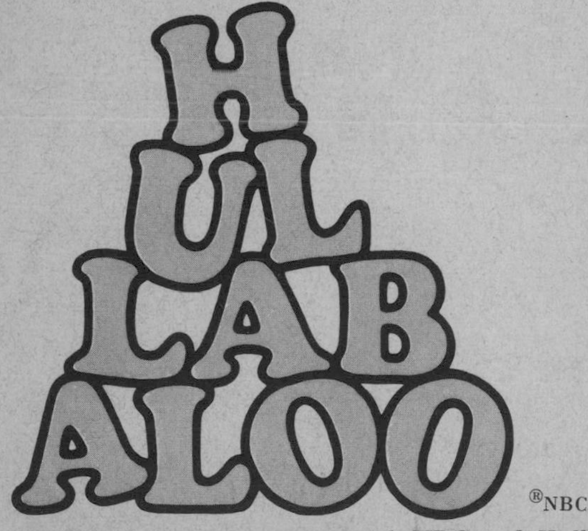

Published by arrangement with NBC and *Hullabaloo.*

A Parallax Book in association with *This Week Magazine.*

SBS SCHOLASTIC BOOK SERVICES
New York • London • Richmond Hill, Ontario

1st printing .... January 1967

Printed in the U.S.A.

Contents

Introduction

Now, right now, something exciting is happening—and you're in on it. Something exciting for anyone who loves dancing—even if you've never touched the stuff before.

What's so great? You'll find it all here in *The Hullabaloo Discothèque Dance Book.*

They're some of the most enjoyable—certainly the most *do*-able—dances ever to come along. Why? Because they're *natural.* Sure there are movements to learn, sometimes even patterns for your feet; but almost anything goes in these dances, so long as you keep loose, and keep the beat.

A Little Background All the Discothèque Dances are imported, mostly from Europe. Except for some of the variations, none of the "official" ones are local products. Even the home-grown Twist doesn't really qualify. The Frug was the first.

Where did the name *discothèque* come from? A *discothèque* is, in France, literally a place where records *(disques)* are stored. It became the term to describe all the places, chic and otherwise, where you can dance to recorded music. The proprietors are happy to save money on orchestras, and the patrons are happy to dance to their favorite records instead of to old-time nightclub bands—even at nightclub prices.

Discothèques have spread all over Europe (there are now even some in the Orient) and all over the U.S.A. Probably half of them are called "something *à go-go,*" following the style set by the first of the important European *discothèques,* Whisky à go-go (Paris, Cannes, Athens, etc.). And what does *à go-go* mean? It's just a combination French/American phrase meaning "a-plenty" or "to spare"—an offshoot of the cry of "Go, man, go go go go" that came with jazz and early rock 'n' roll.

Now, to give a little more credit to the U.S.'s part in all this—

It was, still, that all-American Twist that was the breakthrough—the dance that everybody was doing, talking about, writing about in the papers—not just in the gossip columns, but on the front pages. The Twist was the dance that showed people they could, and should, loosen up and swing.

And now it's the Jerk, the Frug, the Monkey, from Sybil Burton Christopher's *discothèque* Arthur, to the high school gym camouflaged with crepe paper, from the White House to your living room, from Beverly Hills' posh private club, The Daisy, to great big happy HULLABALOO. Everybody's doing it, everybody's loving it.

1-and-2-and-Yeah-Yeah-Yeah The Discothèque Dances really loosen you up. O.K., they wear you out, too—but what a way to go. Whether all the music is exactly to your taste or not, you'll find you won't be able to resist the beat. It'll show. Your foot, your knee, your fingers—something is going to respond to that music, whether you're sitting it out at a chic *discothèque* or waiting for your take-out order of pizza and No-Cal.

Coordination. That's the key. And that *can* be learned. Whether you're a natural athlete or wish you had a remote-control TV so you didn't have to get up to turn down the commercials, you can have fun doing all the dances in this book.

A Discothèque Dance is not just a new step, but a whole new *kind* of dance. If you have never been great at the two-step or the waltz, you can still be great with these. It may just take you a little time: even dance teachers have been known to have trouble. But wait and see. You'll get to feel as if you're just *responding* to the sound of the Top Twenty.

Most of the dances are danced to a steady beat. You can't help hearing the beat, really *feeling* it, and that's what you move to—not to the melody. (You could probably do a fine fox trot to *that*.)

Several Do's and a Don't or Two To start with a "Don't," don't try to learn more than one dance a day. You can check your own progress on charts based on the one shown (using A, B, C, D, and Flunk, school-grade style, or any other system you decide on), daily or weekly, comparing your image in the mirror against the illustrations in this book. But if you can keep time through a whole song doing the Frug—*that's* progress.

Progress Chart

Pattern							
Footwork							
Timing/Rhythm							
Continuity							
Styling							
Confidence							

Basically, this is the chart instructors teaching the Discothèque Dances use to record their students' progress, from lesson to lesson. It's the chart they've used all along for the ballroom dances, but with some changes that will give you some good clues to the *what* and *why* of Discothèque Dances—what makes them different, and why they're fun to do.

1. Continuity is new on the chart. You don't do just one or two dances all evening, or even for the duration of one song, as you could with a fox trot. No matter how terrific you get at, say, the Frug, you can't get out on the dance floor till you've learned at least another couple of dances; you'll get bored, you'll bore your partner, you'll bore anybody who's watching. You've got to be able to go casually from one dance into another—and no matter what your partner does or doesn't do, you can go on to something else whenever you feel like it.

2. Confidence has been on all the charts. You're on your own in a lot of these dances, and although you yourself will be the best judge of how confident you are, others can tell, too. So smile. These dances *are* fun, and you should look as if you are enjoying yourself. Look animated—but if you can't quite manage that sometimes, at least try to look cool. A look of serious concentration (Can't you *always* tell when people are counting 1-2-3-1-2-3 to themselves?) just doesn't go with these dances.

3. Styling is another old standard on the list. This book gives suggestions for where to place your hands, where to move your feet, and how to bend your body. But styling can be a very personal thing, and whatever jerk or jiggle you're comfortable with—try it, and see if it works. There are so many variations possible that almost anything that fits the beat will turn out to be O.K. The best test: Does it feel right? If so—go ahead.

What about the items *missing* from the list? Like . . .

1. Following and Leading Your Partner. Forget it. Except for, say, the Watusi, you hardly ever have to follow or lead your partner, so you can feel freer. Great not to worry about stepping on toes!

2. Posture. If you can call standing with your rear end stuck out, your head forward, and your feet pigeon-toed . . . if you can call that *posture*, then posture counts. But according to what your grade school gym teacher meant by the word, it doesn't matter very much here.

Watusi, anyone? Mouse, Monkey, Freddy? They can't be serious. But that's just the point.

You're going to have a good time even learning the Discothèque Dances. And once you're actually *doing* them—the greatest.

The Frug

1

What's most important here is coordination. The Frug may be a little hard to "get"—but it's one of the most popular, so must be worth getting.

And if you've ever managed to coordinate enough to pat-your-head/rub-your-stomach, you can feel confident about the Frug.

Feet: Rest all your weight on your left foot—as if you were waiting for a bus—with your leg stiff. Let your right knee bend. Feet as close or far apart as you find most comfortable once you get into the movement.

Body: Generally, forward.

Hands: Waist-high.

Basic Movement: Just keeping time with your right knee, bending and straightening as much as possible—as much as the rapid beat of the music will allow.

Note: Most people find that they're most comfortable with their feet just a few inches apart, the right foot just a little more forward than the left.

Styling: Alternate your hands, front and back; when your right hand is in front, your left is in back, two beats each. (Figures 1 and 2)

For girls only—put your wrists, with the palms of your hands in, against your hips.

For either of the above styles, you look to the left when the left hand is forward (two beats) and to the right when the right hand is forward (two beats).

Once you do "get it," you'll find that the overall movement of the Frug comes from your rib cage—*above* the hips.

2

FROM THE FRUG, YOU CAN GO RIGHT TO

The Swim

WHICH IS REALLY JUST A VARIATION OF THE FRUG.

1 2

Feet and Basic Movement: Frug.

Hands: Here's the difference. Your hands do your familiar old swimming strokes: dog paddle (Figures 1 and 2), breast stroke (Figures 3 and 4), back stroke (Figures 5 and 6), etc., four or two beats per movement. If you can swim, you can Swim.

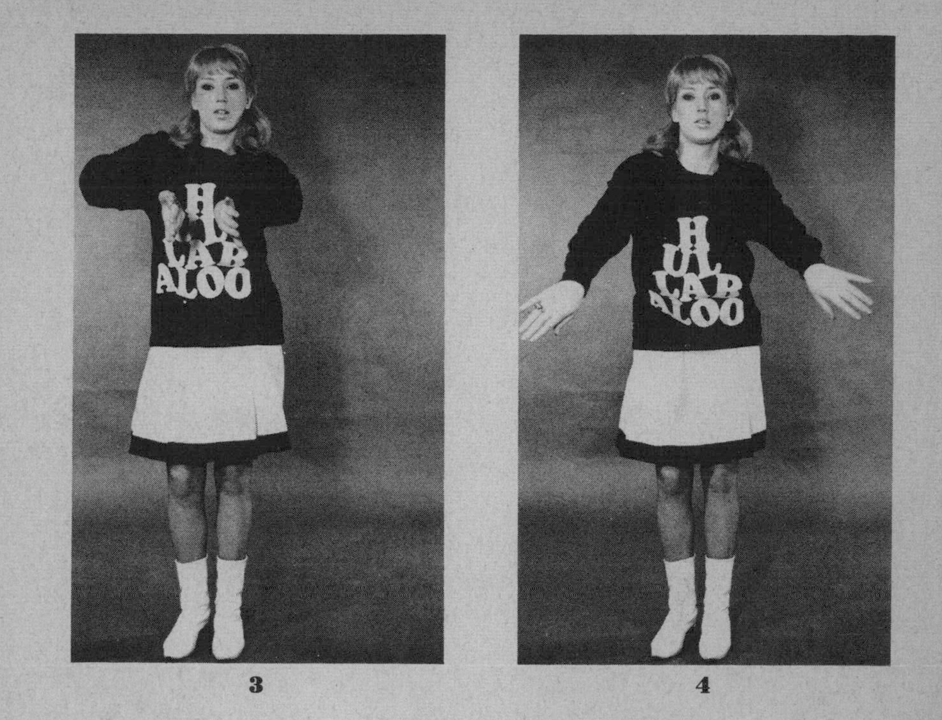

3 4

5

6

2

1

ANOTHER DANCE THAT IS BASICALLY ANOTHER FRUG—WITH A PLUS:

The Bug

You and your partner are doing the Frug. But one of you, say your partner, instead of the usual Frug hand motion, does a shooing motion to the beat of the record—shooing "a bug" away, to the left, to the right.

Suddenly, the shooer "throws it" (the bug) to you and goes back to the Frug hand movements, leaving it up to you to shoo till you feel like throwing it *back*.

Note: You can throw the bug to someone *other* than your partner—at least if you're among friends.

Also, you can use these hand movements with dances other than the Frug.

3

4

5

The Hitchhiker

Feet and Basic Movement: Frug.

Hands: Frug, too, but—with your thumbs up, as if you were hitching a ride. Here, too, as your right hand moves back, you look at it; left hand moves back, look at *it*. (Figures 1 and 2)

1

2

1

2

The Twist

Discothèque Dance or not, it's still donc a lot and, unlike the other dances in this book—and other dances in general—the Twist can be learned in a couple of minutes. All you have to do is master a single trick.

Feet: About five inches apart, weight on the balls of your feet.

Body: Straight, knees "comfortable."

Hands: Waist-high, once you're really doing the dance.

Basic Movement: The learnable trick. Pretend you've stepped out of the shower, holding a towel behind you, your hands thigh-high —and dry your rear.

Another way to get the foot movement: pretend you are putting out a cigarette with your right toe (not the ball of your foot), resting your weight on your (non-moving) left foot—or vice versa, if you prefer. (Figure 1)

Eventually you can alternate to the count of 4, "putting out the cigarette" with your right toe, then switching weight and doing it with your left toe. (Figure 2)

Continued on the next page.

3

4

Or you can (staying in the same basic position) "put cigarettes out" with both feet at once.

You don't really need to progress further than this to do, and enjoy, the Twist.

Whatever method or style you settle on, and once you can give up your "towel" and "cigarette," hands are at waist level. When your knees are to the right, your hands are to the left; knees left, hands right. (Figures 3 and 4)

And when you're comfortable with that much, to a count of 4, bend forward and back—4 counts forward, 4 back, 4 forward, 4 back.

If you want to go further with the Twist, here are some variations:

Variation: Go all the way down and back up, either as your partner does the same or as one of you goes up, the other goes down. (Figures 5 and 6)

Variation: Turning: if you do your Twist with the left foot forward, you turn toward the right, or vice versa. You pivot on the balls of your feet, keeping them basically in place.

Variation: Lift one hand over your head and move it in a circular motion—as if you were going to lasso a bull. (Figures 7 and 8)

You can do practically any of the above in combination with the rest, and you will find other variations that come naturally as you go along.

5

6

7

8

1

2

The Monkey

Feet: About six inches apart, legs straight, knees "locked." They—legs and feet—don't have to do another thing in this dance.

Body: Straight, for the moment.

Basic Movement: Forward and back, from the hips. Achieve it by thrusting either your rear out and back, or your shoulders or chest forward and back. Your head bobs in time.

3

Hands: Hand movements make the dance, here. Held at face level, open, palms out toward your partner, your hands move in a counter-clockwise circle toward your face.

When your right hand is out, your partner's left is out so that you almost, but not quite, touch, palm to palm; and vice versa.

Variation: Try climbing a rope instead.

The Jerk

This is basically the Monkey—but with your arms and hands moving as if you were leading a band—crossing your wrists in front of your chest, then sweeping out—in time, or at half time, with your body movement, to the count of four.

Your hands are up at face level. On count 1, the outward sweep, "push" your hands out into the outward sweep, giving a jerky motion. For a little more style—snap your fingers on the two outward movements—the first and third counts of your hand motion.

1 2

The Boston Monkey

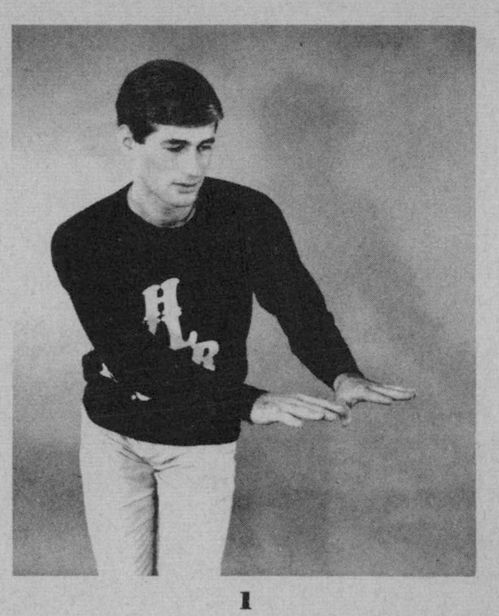

1

Feet: Together, knees bent.

Body: Bent from the waist.

Hands: In front of you, palms down, at waist level.

Movement: Hips to the left, hips to the right.

You push your right hip out, and slightly back, at the same time moving your hands to the left. (Figure 1)

2

You push your left hip out, and slightly back, at the same time moving your hands to the right. (Figure 2)

All done bobbing, Monkey-like.

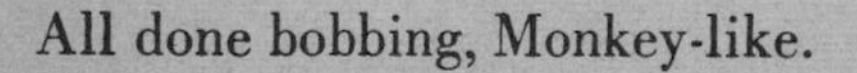

TV STAR SOUPY SALES'S DANCE:

The Mouse

IS ANOTHER MONKEY VARIATION.

What makes the Monkey the Mouse?

Put your thumbs to your ears, wiggle your fingers, put your upper teeth over your lower lip—and keep the beat with your knees. That's the whole Mouse.

1

2

1

The Bird

Feet: A few inches apart; they don't move.

Body: You're bent forward, facing—and close to—your partner. Almost nose-to-nose.

Hands: You keep them on your thighs.

Basic Movement: Your head does it all: move it forward to the right, then to the left, then to the right, to the left, and so on. Just keep repeating.

But watch out! Be sure you and your partner are bobbing to the same count, and are bobbing to the right at the same time and to the left at the same time. Otherwise—head-on (nose-on)collision.

2

ONE OF THE NEW YORK *DISCOTHÈQUES*—WITH JAPANESE DÉCOR AND MENU—HAS HAD A NEW DANCE CREATED ESPECIALLY FOR IT. IT'S REALLY FOR THE GIRLS WHO DANCE IN THE HANGING CAGES, BUT THE PATRONS ARE DOING IT, TOO. THE NAME OF THE *DISCOTHÈQUE*, AND OF THE DANCE IS *THE GINZA*.

2

1

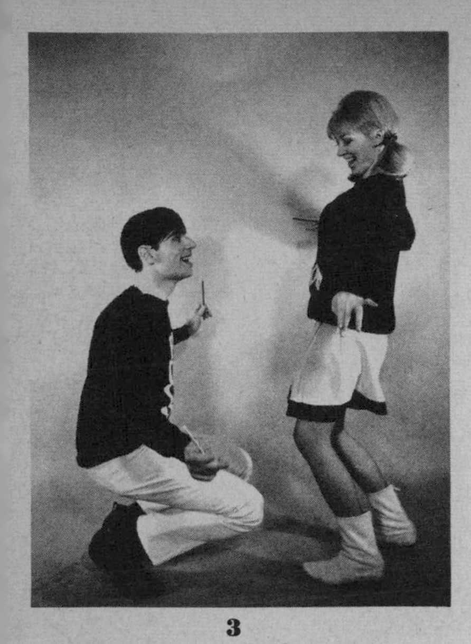

3

4

The Ginza

BASICALLY A MONKEY, BUT:

Hands: Extended, holding chopsticks (or whatever prop you can dig up. Use your imagination.)

Movement: Facing partner, you maintain a Monkey beat but go down, bending from the knees. As you are going back up, your partner is going down. And vice versa.

5

The Mashed Potatoes

Count: Step turn/step turn.

Feet: About a foot apart.

Hands: Waist-high, or higher.

Body: Leaning forward.

Movement: Basically the Roaring Twenties' Charleston "toe swivel," updated for the *discothèques*.

1. Step to the right with your right foot.

2. Place your left toe to the heel of your right foot, simultaneously turning your right heel inward.

Then repeat to the left:

3. Step left.

4. Right toe to left heel as you turn your left heel inward.

2

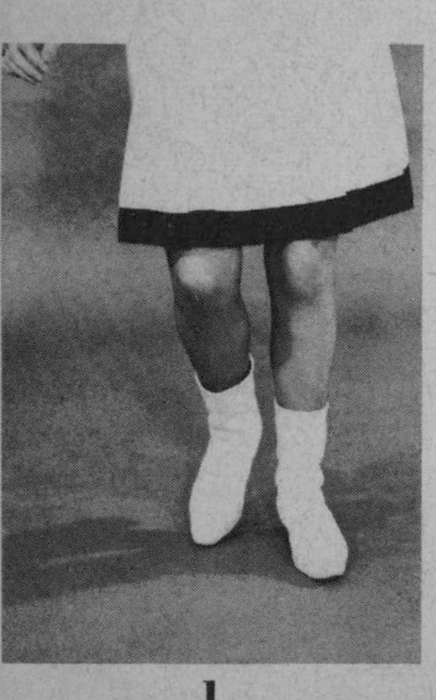

1

3

4

5

Variation: One hand on thigh, one above shoulder level. You can alternate hand positions: right hand up, left hand on hip, and vice versa.

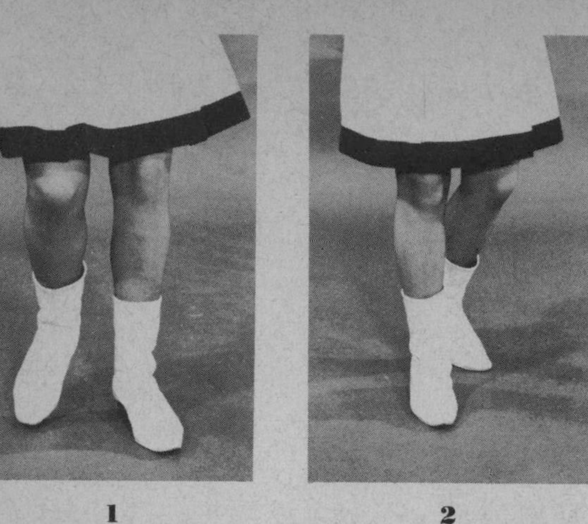

1 2

The Slop

3 4

It is helpful here to think of the

Count: step tap—step tap—walk walk.

Feet: Together.

Hands: Waist level.

Body: Straight.

Movement:

1. Step to the right with your right foot.

2. Bring left foot to right foot in a hard tap on the ball of your foot.

3. Step to the left with your left foot.

4. Bring your right foot to the left in a hard tap.
5. Step back with your right foot.
6. Step back with your left foot.
7. And start all over again—right step, tap left, step left, tap right, walk back right, walk back left. . . .

Lean forward from the waist on the walk steps.

Variation: You can do this turning—on any count—as you would a two step or waltz.

Variation: Instead of bringing one foot to the other in the tap (counts 2 and 4, above), bring the "tap foot" toe to the heel of the other foot.

6

5

The Pachanga

Although it's not really in the Discothèque Dance category, the basic Pachanga can be done as part of the Slop, to a one-two count.

The step/tap of the Slop is replaced by a stomp/swivel:

1. Stomp your left foot.

2. Then turn your left toe out.

3. Stomp your right foot.

4. Turn your right toe out.

Repeat, adding a little style by emphasizing the hip motion.

1

2

Table Talk

When the dance floor is too crowded, or your legs are too tired, here, for sitting it out, is *Table Talk* (created specially for this book): Every movement is to two beats—half time. Just stay seated where you are and do the following hand/arm movements, each to two beats (half time):

1. Stretch right arm in front of you, hand palm down, parallel to the table top.

2. Same for left arm.

Continued on next page.

3

4

3. Right hand to left shoulder.

4. Left hand to right shoulder.

5. Left hand to left knee.

6. Right hand to right knee.

5

6

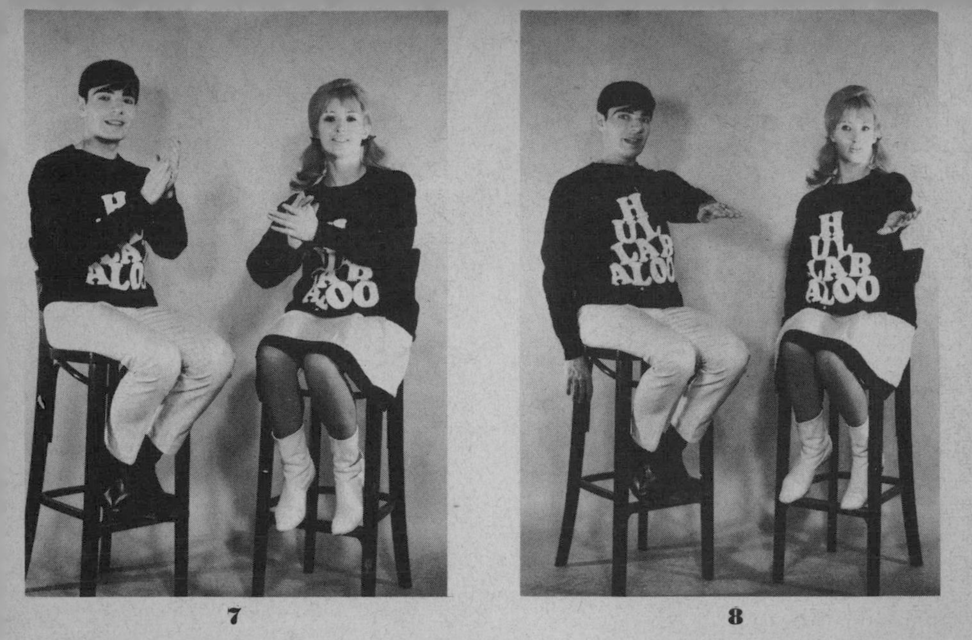

7 8

9 10

7. Clap twice.

8. Stretch left arm in front of you, hand palm down, and *look* at hand as you put it out.

9. Same for right.

10. Turn left palm up—and look.

Continued on next page.

11. Right palm up. Look.

12. Clap twice.

13. Right fist to left elbow, tap twice.

14. Left fist to right elbow, tap twice.

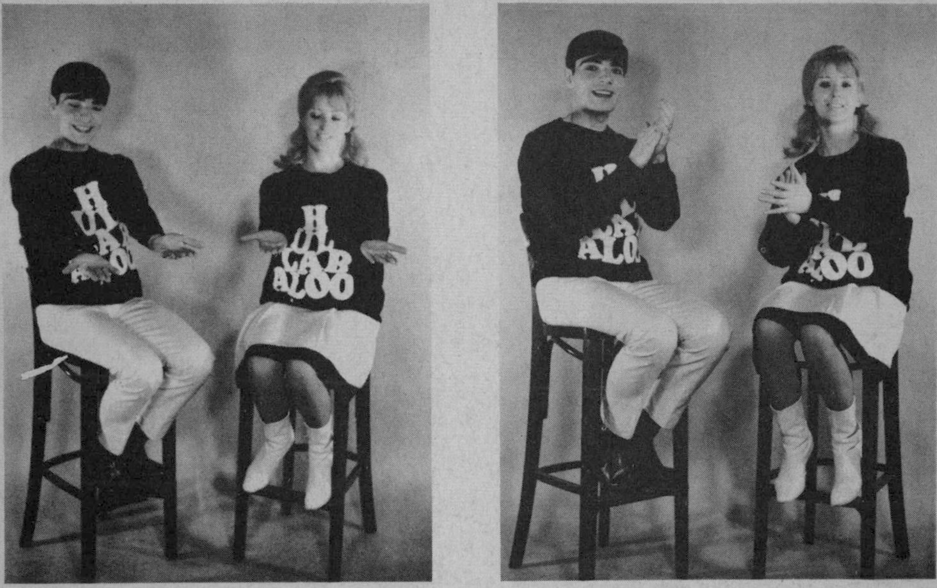

11

12

13

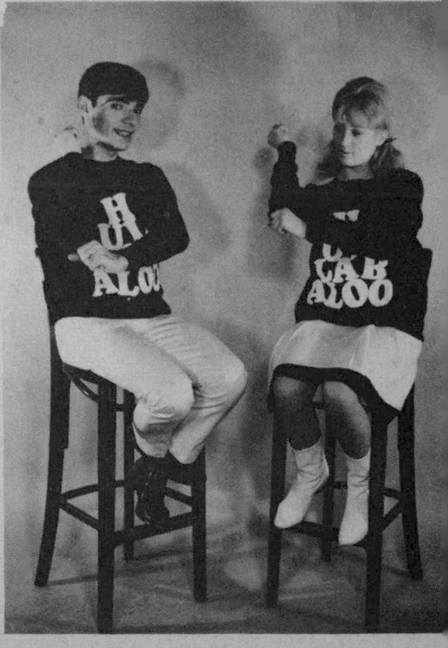

14

15

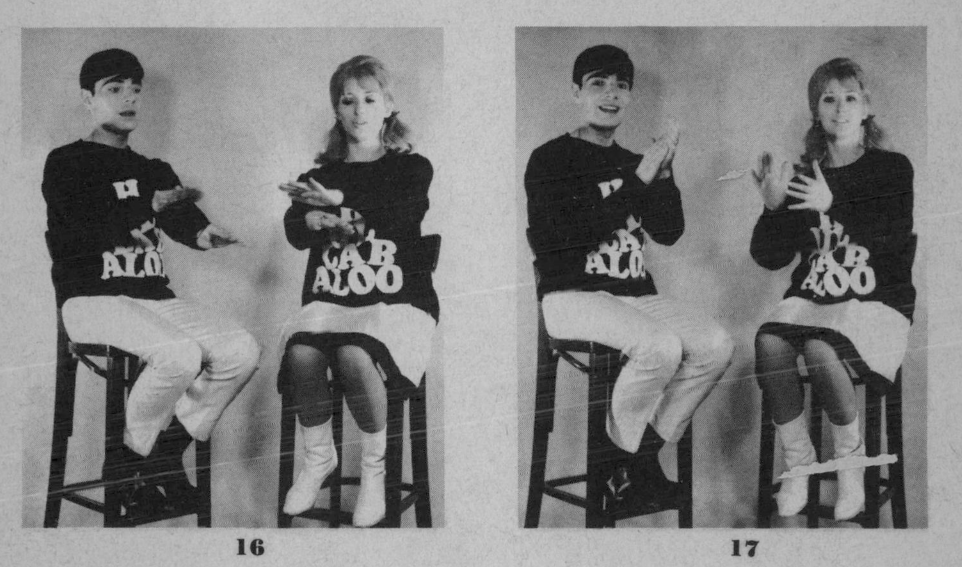

16 17

15. Left hand passes over right twice, 1 beat per pass, in front of you, close.

16. Right hand over left, twice.

17. Clap twice.

It's easier to learn the pattern than it looks. You can make up as many variations as you wish, with partners following each other a beat late, à la Simon Sez.

IN KEEPING WITH THE SPREADING POPULARITY OF THE DISCOTHÈQUE DANCES, A BRAND-NEW DANCE HAS BEEN CREATED FOR THIS BOOK, WITH AN INDIAN FLAVOR AND A *DISCOTHÈQUE* FLAIR.

The Bombay

1 2

Feet: Turned out, as far as you can, heel to heel.

Body: Straight; stand in front or in back of your partner.

Arms: Outstretched, or bent at the elbows, hands out flat, palms up.

Movement: Bend side to side from the waist. Your partner should be doing the same, but bending to the left when you are bending to the right, and vice versa. (Figures 1 and 2) (For a head-on view, see Figure 3.)

Variation: Face partner and arch arms over head; move your head left and right, as far as you can *without turning it to either side*. (See Figure 4)

3

4

The Watusi

At least that's what they call it in New York; but it's also the Wobble, the Waddle, the Madison, and in France, *Le* Madison.

Just about the only one of the Discothèque Dances that you must do with your partner—that is, where you *follow* each other.

Count: slow—quick quick tap/slow—quick quick tap.

Feet: Together.

1

2

Body: Bent a little, from the waist, head forward; you face your partner (the photos are front view to show the steps more clearly).

Hands: Waist-high, or at sides with hands out, palms down.

Basic Movement: Sideways, to the count of four (ONE-2-3-4): LEFT right left tap/RIGHT left right tap for the man, and the opposite for the woman, then in reverse.

3

4

Woman

1. Step to the right with your right foot.

2. Bring left foot next to right.

3. Step to the right with your right foot.

4. Bring your left foot to your right in a hard tap with the ball of the foot—either next to or to the heel of your right foot. And clap as you tap.

Go straight into the same pattern but to the left side, so your left foot goes straight from the tap to a step left. See following.

Man

1. Step to the left with your left foot.

2. Bring your right foot next to the left.

3. Step to the left with your left foot.

4. Bring your right foot to your left in a hard tap with the ball of the foot—either next to or to the heel of your right foot. And clap as you tap.

Go straight into the same pattern but to the right, so your right foot goes straight from the tap into a step right. You're now going into the pattern given for your partner.

Continued on next page.

Whoever starts first is the leader, really. And it can (and should) turn into a group dance—not just where you know all the other dancers, but even in a *discothèque,* with a caller calling the variations, square-dance style.

The "called" variations all have to do with the hands—and with your imaginativeness.

Popeye, or the Sightseer: Looking right, with your right hand over your eyes and your left on your hip; then looking left, with your left hand over your eyes and your right on your hip; and repeat. (Figure 5)

Rowing the Boat: Hands reach forward and pull back the oars. (Figure 6)

Dean Martin: What else? . . . (Figure 7)

Dracula (Figure 8), *Sammy Davis, Jr., Jayne Mansfield*—anyone or anything you can think of to pantomime.

5

6

7

8

Variation: Do the steps forward and back instead of sideways.

Woman

1. Right foot forward.

2. Left foot forward and left.

3. Right foot forward and right.

4. You end up with your feet apart—and you clap.

Man

1. Left foot forward.

2. Right foot forward and right.

3. Left foot forward and left.

4. You end up with your feet apart—and you clap.

Repeat the same pattern, always starting with the same foot. You can just keep going in one direction till you run out of space, or change directions when you wish.

The Pony

Count: ONE-2-3/ONE-2-3/walk walk (RIGHT left right/RIGHT left right/right left).

Feet: Together, to start (they move a lot, but in place, pretty much).

Hands: Waist-high, palms down, in front of you (next to each other).

1

Basic Movement: (Figure 1)

1. Step down with your right foot.
2. Step down with your left foot.
3. Step down with your right.
4. Step down with your left foot.
5. Step down with your right foot.
6. Step down with your left.
7. Step with the left foot.
8. Step with the right foot.

2

3

Stress steps 1 and 4, and try to get a little jump into this so that there's vertical movement, as in the Samba. While practicing, try making believe you're jumping over something (something small).

If you're practicing with a partner, put your hands on each others' shoulders to get the feeling of the up-and-down motion.

You just keep repeating the above pattern, but can do the following variations:

Variation: Omit the two walk steps (in place) and just go right and left, shuffling your feet. The girls in the *discothèque* cages use this for resting up.

Variation: Hands can do a dog paddle, or as if holding a pony's reins. This looks best for getting across the Pony idea. (Figure 2)

Variation: Turn, keeping the beat. (Figure 3)

UP FROM THE SOUTH FLIES

The Buzzard

IN WHICH YOU . . . IMITATE A BUZZARD

Feet: A few inches apart; they stay in place.

Arms: Outstretched, of course —they're your wings.

Body: Bent from the waist, head forward.

Movement: Bending one knee, then the other, alternately, you wave your arms gracefully. Up and down, up and down, sideways —in flight. There's sort of a hula feeling to the arm motion.

You're lovely.

2

1

3

4

5

6

The Bossa Nova

This Brazilian-type dance is not one of the real Discothèque Dances, but is played a lot with them as a sort of interlude or break.

The music you dance the Bossa Nova to is a cross between Samba and Rumba, with the styling of both: the vertical motion of the Samba and the Cuban (hip) motion of the Rumba.

The tempo here is a little slower than that in the Discothèque Dances. The Bossa Nova is done smoothly and, unlike the other "tap" steps in this book, the tap here is a light one.

Also different from most of the Discothèque Dances: you follow your partner, in regular dance position. Remember *that?*

Count: step-tap/step-tap/step-tap/step-tap.

Feet: Together.

Movement: Basically, a shift of weight from one foot to the other, in a little back-and-forth and side-to-side pattern.

1

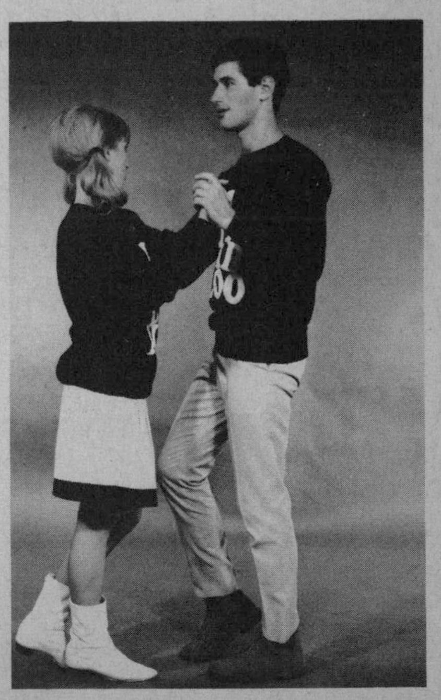

2

Man

1. Step forward with your left foot.

2. Tap with right (toe).

3. Step back with your right foot.

4. Tap with your left (toe).

5. Step to the side with your left foot.

6. Tap with your right.

7. Step to the side with your right foot.

8. Tap with your left.

And repeat.

Woman

1. Step back with your right foot.

2. Tap with your left (toe).

3. Step forward with your left foot.

4. Tap with your right (toe).

5. Step to the side with your right foot.

6. Tap with your left.

7. Step to the side with your left foot.

8. Tap with your right.

And repeat.

3

4

Continued on next page.

Variation: A walk-around—The man keeps the 1-2 (step-tap) beat, side-to-side only. As he does the first *left* toe tap, he lifts his left hand and the girl goes into a (complete) turn to the count of

1—tap/2—tap/3—tap/4—tap/5—tap/6—tap

On the count of six, she should be back in position, facing partner.

Then, back into the basic Bossa Nova.

5

6

7

The Freddy

This was "created" by the singing group, Freddy and the Dreamers, who do it as they sing. On the dance floor, you do it facing your partner; you don't need to sing.

Count: A very even 1 - 2 - 3 - 4 .

Body: Straight.

Feet: Together.

Hands: At sides.

Basic Movement: Leaning your body side to side, in one place, but . . .

1

2

4

3

Woman

1. Raise your right arm straight out to the right; at the same time, raise your right leg out to the right AND lean your body to the left, so all your weight is *really* on your left leg.

2. Back to original position—"at attention."

3. Raise your left arm and left leg out, and lean right.

4. Back to original position.

And repeat: right arm and leg out, lean left; left arm and leg out, lean right.

Continued on next page.

5

6

Man

You and your partner can do this in the same direction: when she is raising her right arm and leg, you are raising your left.

But you can also do it in opposite directions, with both of you going to your right at the same time, to your left at the same time. (Figure 5)

And do it in front of each other (Figure 6), or back to back for variety.

Tee-hee.

FROM WHERE THE RUM COMES FROM COMES

The Ska (or Jamaican Ska)

Count: A simple 1-2, 1-2: step-tap, step-tap.

Feet: Together.

Body: Straight.

Hands: Crossed in front of you, waist level.

1

2

Basic Movement:

1. Step to the right, swinging hands out and bending 'way over from the waist. (Figure 1)

2. Bring left foot in back of right in a tap, bending your knees and shifting your body weight backward. Your hands come back in front of you, crossed. (Figure 2)

Repeat to the left side:

1. Step to the left, swinging hands out and bending forward.

2. Bring your right foot in back of the left in a tap, bending your knees and shifting your body weight backward. Your hands come back in front of you, crossed.

Continued on next page.

Variation: Hands can be as if you were rowing a boat: pull forward on the oars when you're bending forward on the first count; pull backwards—till your hands are stretched out behind you—on the second (tap) count. (Figures 3 and 4)

Variation: Hands can be climbing a rope.

You can go nicely from the Ska into the Frug, moving your right foot forward, putting your weight on your right, and keeping the rhythm with your knee (see page 12).

3

4

5

Recommended Frug variation for use with the Ska:

Washing Clothes:

Left hand is holding washboard, right is scrubbing. When you shift your weight to your left leg and keep time with your right knee, let your right hand hold the washboard, and your left hand scrub. Best to count of 4. (Figure 5)

1

The Bostella

The music for this is Mexican Hat Dance music, and you can do the Mexican Hat Dance steps to it, too. You can really do anything else you care to do, so long as it fits the beat and is very lively.

Your hands can go on your hips and/or over your head; you can hold one of your partner's hands, or both, or not hold hands at all, though it may be helpful to "anchor" yourself for the ending—which is really the whole point of the Bostella. *Continued on page 64.*

2

3

4

5

Everyone falls down!

In Paris *discothèques,* where the Bostella started, most people wear practical-for-falling-on-the-floor black. But the really *chic* ones do the wild thing: they wear—but of course—white.

Word of warning: cut in at your own risk!

6